This planner belongs to

_____

Growing in Grace

2016

16-MONTH
WEEKLY PLANNER

BELLE CITY GIFTS

SEPTEMBER 2015						
S	M	T	W	T	F	S
		1	2	3	4	5
6	7	8	9	10	11	12
13	14	15	16	17	18	19
20	21	22	23	24	25	26
27	28	29	30			

OCTOBER 2015						
S	M	T	W	T	F	S
				1	2	3
4	5	6	7	8	9	10
11	12	13	14	15	16	17
18	19	20	21	22	23	24
25	26	27	28	29	30	31

NOVEMBER 2015						
S	M	T	W	T	F	S
1	2	3	4	5	6	7
8	9	10	11	12	13	14
15	16	17	18	19	20	21
22	23	24	25	26	27	28
29	30					

DECEMBER 2015						
S	M	T	W	T	F	S
		1	2	3	4	5
6	7	8	9	10	11	12
13	14	15	16	17	18	19
20	21	22	23	24	25	26
27	28	29	30	31		

JANUARY 2016						
S	M	T	W	T	F	S
					1	2
3	4	5	6	7	8	9
10	11	12	13	14	15	16
17	18	19	20	21	22	23
24	25	26	27	28	29	30
31						

FEBRUARY 2016						
S	M	T	W	T	F	S
	1	2	3	4	5	6
7	8	9	10	11	12	13
14	15	16	17	18	19	20
21	22	23	24	25	26	27
28	29					

MARCH 2016						
S	M	T	W	T	F	S
		1	2	3	4	5
6	7	8	9	10	11	12
13	14	15	16	17	18	19
20	21	22	23	24	25	26
27	28	29	30	31		

APRIL 2016						
S	M	T	W	T	F	S
					1	2
3	4	5	6	7	8	9
10	11	12	13	14	15	16
17	18	19	20	21	22	23
24	25	26	27	28	29	30

MAY 2016						
S	M	T	W	T	F	S
1	2	3	4	5	6	7
8	9	10	11	12	13	14
15	16	17	18	19	20	21
22	23	24	25	26	27	28
29	30	31				

JUNE 2016						
S	M	T	W	T	F	S
			1	2	3	4
5	6	7	8	9	10	11
12	13	14	15	16	17	18
19	20	21	22	23	24	25
26	27	28	29	30		

JULY 2016						
S	M	T	W	T	F	S
					1	2
3	4	5	6	7	8	9
10	11	12	13	14	15	16
17	18	19	20	21	22	23
24	25	26	27	28	29	30
31						

AUGUST 2016						
S	M	T	W	T	F	S
	1	2	3	4	5	6
7	8	9	10	11	12	13
14	15	16	17	18	19	20
21	22	23	24	25	26	27
28	29	30	31			

SEPTEMBER 2016						
S	M	T	W	T	F	S
				1	2	3
4	5	6	7	8	9	10
11	12	13	14	15	16	17
18	19	20	21	22	23	24
25	26	27	28	29	30	

OCTOBER 2016						
S	M	T	W	T	F	S
						1
2	3	4	5	6	7	8
9	10	11	12	13	14	15
16	17	18	19	20	21	22
23	24	25	26	27	28	29
30	31					

NOVEMBER 2016						
S	M	T	W	T	F	S
		1	2	3	4	5
6	7	8	9	10	11	12
13	14	15	16	17	18	19
20	21	22	23	24	25	26
27	28	29	30			

DECEMBER 2016						
S	M	T	W	T	F	S
				1	2	3
4	5	6	7	8	9	10
11	12	13	14	15	16	17
18	19	20	21	22	23	24
25	26	27	28	29	30	31

Introduction

Having trouble fitting everything in your day?
Based on our devotional journal *Growing in Grace*,
this 16-month planner makes getting organized
simple and inspiring.

Each beautifully designed page blends practical
weekly plans with motivating thoughts and verses.
High-quality paper allows you to confidently write
reminders, schedules, and personal notes in the
space provided. You can also view this year and
next at a convenient glance.

Be encouraged, stay organized and realize that
God is able to make all grace abound to you, so
that you can grow and prosper in every good work!

September

2015

Each second you had was a gift

Each second that came and then went

It hoped it would be met with courage

It hoped it would be wisely spent

31 million seconds now leave you

31 million more on their way

What will you wisely choose to accomplish

with your 86,000 today?

S	M	T	W	T	F	S
		1	2	3	4	5
6	7	8	9	10	11	12
13	14	15	16	17	18	19
20	21	22	23	24	25	26
27	28	29	30			

Live wisely among those who are not believers, and make the most of every opportunity.

COLOSSIANS 4:5 NLT

Consecrate yourselves, for tomorrow the
LORD will do amazing things among you.

Joshua 3:5 NIV

September

31 Monday

_____
_____
_____
_____
_____

1 Tuesday

_____
_____
_____
_____
_____

2 Wednesday

_____
_____
_____
_____
_____

Thursday 3

Friday 4

Saturday 5

Sunday 6

$\mathcal{G}$od never said that the journey would be easy,
but He did say that the arrival would be worthwhile.

MAX LUCADO

We are not saying that we can do this work ourselves. It is God who makes us able to do all that we do.

2 Corinthians 3:5 NCV

September

7 Monday *Labor Day*

_____

_____

_____

_____

8 Tuesday

_____

_____

_____

_____

9 Wednesday

_____

_____

_____

_____

Thursday 10

_____

_____

_____

_____

_____

Friday 11

_____

_____

_____

_____

_____

Saturday 12

_____

_____

Rosh Hashanah begins **Sunday** 13

_____

_____

_____

You cannot always wait for the perfect time.
Sometimes you must dare to jump.

My grace is sufficient for you,
for my power is made perfect in weakness.

2 Corinthians 12:9 ESV

September

14   Monday

_____
_____
_____
_____
_____

15   Tuesday   *Rosh Hashanah ends*

_____
_____
_____
_____
_____

16   Wednesday

_____
_____
_____
_____
_____

Thursday 17

Friday 18

Saturday 19

Sunday 20

Success is not final; failure is not fatal.

It is the courage to continue that counts.

WINSTON CHURCHILL

"I am the Light of the world; he who follows Me will not walk in the darkness, but will have the Light of life."

John 8:12 NASB

September

21 Monday

22 Tuesday *Yom Kippur begins*

23 Wednesday *Autumnal Equinox / Yom Kippur ends*

Thursday 24

Friday 25

Saturday 26

Sunday 27

The ultimate measure of a man is not where he stands in moments of comfort and convenience, but where he stands at times of challenge and controversy.

MARTIN LUTHER KING JR.

October
2015

I don't know what I ever did to win the love you give

But without what I've grown to know I surely could not live

You fill up all my senses when you touch my face, my skin

And love the me I am today despite the me I've been

S	M	T	W	T	F	S
				1	2	3
4	5	6	7	8	9	10
11	12	13	14	15	16	17
18	19	20	21	22	23	24
25	26	27	28	29	30	31

We love because he first loved us.

1 JOHN 4:19 ESV

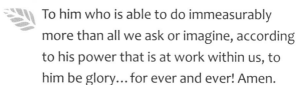

To him who is able to do immeasurably more than all we ask or imagine, according to his power that is at work within us, to him be glory… for ever and ever! Amen.

Ephesians 3:20-21 NIV

September/October

28 Monday

_____

_____

_____

_____

_____

29 Tuesday

_____

_____

_____

_____

_____

30 Wednesday

_____

_____

_____

_____

_____

Thursday 1

Friday 2

Saturday 3

Sunday 4

Anxiety does not empty tomorrow of its sorrows,

but only empties today of its strength.

CHARLES SPURGEON

Jesus Christ is the same yesterday and today and forever.

Hebrews 13:8 NASB

October

5 Monday

6 Tuesday

7 Wednesday

Thursday 8

_____
_____
_____
_____

Friday 9

_____
_____
_____
_____

Saturday 10

_____
_____

Sunday 11

_____
_____
_____

God never hurries. There are no deadlines against which
he must work. Only to know this is to quiet our spirits
and relax our nerves.

A.W. TOZER

The LORD always keeps his promises;
he is gracious in all he does.

Psalm 145:13 NLT

October

12   **Monday**   *Columbus Day*

13   **Tuesday**

14   **Wednesday**

Thursday 15

_____
_____
_____
_____
_____

Friday 16

_____
_____
_____
_____
_____

Saturday 17

_____
_____
_____

Sunday 18

_____
_____
_____

*P*rayer puts God's work in his hands and keeps it there.

E.M. BOUNDS

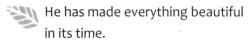 He has made everything beautiful
in its time.

Ecclesiastes 3:11 NIV

October

19 Monday

_____
_____
_____
_____
_____

20 Tuesday

_____
_____
_____
_____
_____

21 Wednesday

_____
_____
_____
_____
_____

Thursday 22

Friday 23

Saturday 24

Sunday 25

It takes time to be a success, but time is all it takes.

The LORD is near to all who call on him,
to all who call on him in truth.

Psalm 145:18 NIV

October/November

26 Monday

_____

_____

_____

_____

27 Tuesday

_____

_____

_____

_____

28 Wednesday

_____

_____

_____

_____

Thursday 29

_____
_____
_____
_____
_____

Friday 30

_____
_____
_____
_____
_____

Saturday 31

_____
_____
_____

Daylight Saving Time ends **Sunday** 1

_____
_____
_____

God loves each of us as if there were only one of us.

AUGUSTINE

November

2015

What if I dared

to not be compared

to a person a place or a thing?

And what if I chose

when those feelings arose

to be happy, content and then sing?

S	M	T	W	T	F	S
1	2	3	4	5	6	7
8	9	10	11	12	13	14
15	16	17	18	19	20	21
22	23	24	25	26	27	28
29	30					

Godliness with contentment is great gain.

1 TIMOTHY 6:6 NIV

"Behold, I am with you always,
to the end of the age."

Matthew 28:20 NIV

November

2 Monday

---

3 Tuesday *Election Day*

---

4 Wednesday

Thursday 5

_____
_____
_____
_____
_____

Friday 6

_____
_____
_____
_____

Saturday 7

_____
_____
_____

Sunday 8

_____
_____
_____

*When we lose one blessing, another is often most
unexpectedly given in its place.*

C.S. LEWIS

From his abundance we have all received
one gracious blessing after another.

John 1:16 NLT

November

9 Monday

10 Tuesday

11 Wednesday *Veterans' Day*

Thursday 12

_____
_____
_____
_____
_____

Friday 13

_____
_____
_____
_____

Saturday 14

_____
_____
_____

Sunday 15

_____
_____
_____

I have too many flaws to be perfect.

But I have too many blessings to be ungrateful.

Do not be anxious about anything, but in every situation, by prayer and petition, with thanksgiving, present your requests to God.

Philippians 4:6 NIV

November

16 Monday

_____

_____

_____

_____

_____

17 Tuesday

_____

_____

_____

_____

_____

18 Wednesday

_____

_____

_____

_____

_____

Thursday 19

Friday 20

Saturday 21

Sunday 22

Happy is the person who learns to wait when they pray because God's time is the best time.

The LORD directs the steps of the godly.
He delights in every detail of their lives.

Psalm 37:23 NLT

November

23 Monday

24 Tuesday

25 Wednesday

Thanksgiving Day **Thursday** 26

Friday 27

Saturday 28

First Sunday of Advent **Sunday** 29

_L_ife itself can't give you joy, unless you really will it.

Life just gives you time and space; it's up to you to fill it.

December
2015

With all His homes in heav'n and earth

Christ searches for one more

The irony: we hold the key

that lets Him in the door

S	M	T	W	T	F	S
		1	2	3	4	5
6	7	8	9	10	11	12
13	14	15	16	17	18	19
20	21	22	23	24	25	26
27	28	29	30	31		

Even more than all this, clothe yourself in love. Love is what holds you all together in perfect unity.

COLOSSIANS 3:14 NCV

There is a time for everything,
and everything on earth has its special season.

Ecclesiastes 3:1 NCV

November/December

30 Monday

_____
_____
_____
_____

1 Tuesday

_____
_____
_____
_____

2 Wednesday

_____
_____
_____
_____

_____
_____
_____
_____
_____

Friday 4

_____
_____
_____
_____

Saturday 5

_____
_____

Sunday 6

_____
_____
_____

Everyone wants happiness.

No one wants pain.

But you can't have a rainbow,

without a little rain.

Let us then approach God's throne of grace with confidence, so that we may receive mercy and find grace to help us in our time of need.

Hebrews 4:16 NIV

December

7 Monday *Hanukkah begins*

8 Tuesday

9 Wednesday

Thursday 10

_____

_____

_____

_____

Friday 11

_____

_____

_____

_____

Saturday 12

_____

_____

_____

Sunday 13

_____

_____

_____

Long-lasting victory can never be separated from a

long-lasting stand on the foundation of the cross.

WATCHMAN NEE

I am confident of this very thing, that He who began a good work in you will perfect it until the day of Christ Jesus.

Philippians 1:6 NASB

December

14 Monday *Hanukkah ends*

15 Tuesday

16 Wednesday

Thursday 17

Friday 18

Saturday 19

Sunday 20

Sometimes God works secretly and behind the scenes, but he will reveal his work to us when the time is right.

"If you remain in me and my words remain in you, you may ask for anything you want, and it will be granted!"

John 15:7 NLT

December

21 Monday

_____
_____
_____
_____
_____

22 Tuesday *Winter Solstice*

_____
_____
_____
_____
_____

23 Wednesday

_____
_____
_____
_____
_____

Christmas Eve **Thursday** 24

_____
_____
_____
_____

Christmas Day **Friday** 25

_____
_____
_____
_____

Saturday 26

_____
_____
_____

Sunday 27

_____
_____
_____

Confidence is not based on you having all the resources needed to take care of yourself; confidence is based upon the truth that God is faithful.

Sunshine is sweet;
it is good to see the light of day.
People ought to enjoy every day of their lives,
no matter how long they live.

Ecclesiastes 11:7-8 NCV

December/January

28 Monday

_____
_____
_____
_____

29 Tuesday

_____
_____
_____
_____

30 Wednesday

_____
_____
_____
_____

New Year's Eve **Thursday** 31

New Year's Day **Friday** 1

Saturday 2

Sunday 3

Today is the yesterday you worried about tomorrow.

January

2016

I need to be more disciplined

I need a new routine

My flesh, though, is not interested

in what that just might mean

If order's in my schedule, though

my flesh will learn the drill

And if I'll bridle whims and grow

my heart will train my will

S	M	T	W	T	F	S
					1	2
3	4	5	6	7	8	9
10	11	12	13	14	15	16
17	18	19	20	21	22	23
24	25	26	27	28	29	30
31						

For the moment all discipline seems painful rather than pleasant, but later it yields the peaceful fruit of righteousness to those who have been trained by it.

HEBREWS 12:10-11 NLT

May he give you the power to accomplish all
the good things your faith prompts you to do.

2 Thessalonians 1:11 NLT

January

4   Monday

_____
_____
_____
_____
_____

5   Tuesday

_____
_____
_____
_____

6   Wednesday

_____
_____
_____
_____

Thursday 7

Friday 8

Saturday 9

Sunday 10

Time spent in prayer is never wasted.

FRANCOIS FENELON

Be on guard. Stand firm in the faith.
Be courageous. Be strong.
And do everything with love.

1 Corinthians 16:13-14 NLT

January

11 Monday

_____
_____
_____
_____

12 Tuesday

_____
_____
_____
_____

13 Wednesday

_____
_____
_____
_____

Never do tomorrow what you can do today;

procrastination is the thief of time.

Let the beauty of the LORD our God be upon us,
And establish the work of our hands for us.

Psalm 90:17 NKJV

January

18 Monday *Martin Luther King Day*

_____
_____
_____
_____

19 Tuesday

_____
_____
_____
_____

20 Wednesday

_____
_____
_____
_____

Thursday 21

_____

_____

_____

_____

Friday 22

_____

_____

_____

_____

Saturday 23

_____

_____

Sunday 24

_____

_____

_____

God's purpose for today's events may not be seen until tomorrow.

Be sure to use the abilities God has given you.

1 Timothy 4:14 TLB

January

25 Monday

_____

_____

_____

_____

26 Tuesday

_____

_____

_____

_____

27 Wednesday

_____

_____

_____

_____

_____

Thursday 28

_____

_____

_____

_____

Friday 29

_____

_____

_____

_____

Saturday 30

_____

_____

Sunday 31

_____

_____

_____

Like winter snow on summer lawn,

time past is time gone.

February

2016

Today, oh God, I vow to put my heart into Your hands

and humbly plead for You to knead it 'til it understands

That words alone cannot fulfill the duties that are mine

But virtue too, toward man and You, is what I must combine

So give me eyes to see my face and ears to hear my words

That I might judge myself as pure so I can rest assured

S	M	T	W	T	F	S
	1	2	3	4	5	6
7	8	9	10	11	12	13
14	15	16	17	18	19	20
21	22	23	24	25	26	27
28	29					

Because you have these blessings, do your best to add these things to your lives: to your faith, add goodness; and to your goodness, add knowledge.

2 PETER 1:5 NCV

Humble yourselves in the sight of the Lord, and He will lift you up.

James 4:10 NKJV

February

1 Monday

2 Tuesday *Groundhog Day*

3 Wednesday

Thursday 4

_____

_____

_____

_____

Friday 5

_____

_____

_____

_____

Saturday 6

_____

_____

_____

Sunday 7

_____

_____

_____

Humility is displacement of self

by the enthronement of God.

ANDREW MURRAY

Stand firm. Let nothing move you.
Always give yourselves fully to the
work of the Lord, because you know
that your labor in the Lord is not in vain.

1 Corinthians 15:58 NIV

February

8   Monday

_____
_____
_____
_____
_____

9   Tuesday

_____
_____
_____
_____
_____

10   Wednesday   *Ash Wednesday*

_____
_____
_____
_____

Thursday 11

_____
_____
_____
_____
_____

Friday 12

_____
_____
_____
_____

Saturday 13

_____
_____
_____

Valentine's Day **Sunday** 14

_____
_____
_____

*Time is lost when we have not lived a full human life,
time unenriched by experience, creative endeavor,
enjoyment, and suffering.*

DIETRICH BONHOEFFER

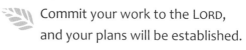

Commit your work to the LORD,
and your plans will be established.

Proverbs 16:3 ESV

February

15 Monday *Presidents' Day*

_____
_____
_____
_____

16 Tuesday

_____
_____
_____
_____

17 Wednesday

_____
_____
_____
_____
_____

Thursday 18

Friday 19

Saturday 20

Sunday 21

Whatever you undertake, act with prudence, and consider the consequences.

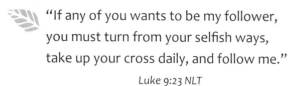

"If any of you wants to be my follower,
you must turn from your selfish ways,
take up your cross daily, and follow me."

Luke 9:23 NLT

February

22 Monday

_____
_____
_____
_____

23 Tuesday

_____
_____
_____
_____

24 Wednesday

_____
_____
_____
_____
_____

Thursday 25

Friday 26

Saturday 27

Sunday 28

It's not about having time. It's about making time.

March

2016

My yesterdays are in you,

they see me through today

You'll carry my tomorrows,

no matter what they weigh

S	M	T	W	T	F	S
		1	2	3	4	5
6	7	8	9	10	11	12
13	14	15	16	17	18	19
20	21	22	23	24	25	26
27	28	29	30	31		

Don't worry about tomorrow, for tomorrow will bring its own worries. Today's trouble is enough for today.

MATTHEW 6:34 NLT

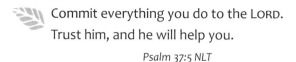 Commit everything you do to the LORD.
Trust him, and he will help you.

Psalm 37:5 NLT

February/March

29 Monday

_____
_____
_____
_____

1 Tuesday

_____
_____
_____
_____

2 Wednesday

_____
_____
_____
_____
_____

_____

_____

_____

_____

_____

Friday 4

_____

_____

_____

_____

Saturday 5

_____

_____

_____

Sunday 6

_____

_____

_____

To worry about tomorrow steals the joy from today.

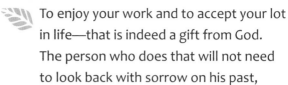 To enjoy your work and to accept your lot
in life—that is indeed a gift from God.
The person who does that will not need
to look back with sorrow on his past,
for God gives him joy.

Ecclesiastes 5:20 TLB

March

7 Monday

8 Tuesday

9 Wednesday

Thursday 10

_____

_____

_____

_____

_____

Friday 11

_____

_____

_____

_____

_____

Saturday 12

_____

_____

_____

Daylight Saving Time begins **Sunday** 13

_____

_____

_____

The present is the only time in which any duty

may be done or grace received.

C.S. LEWIS

In all the work you are doing, work the best
you can. Work as if you were doing it for
the Lord, not for people.

Colossians 3:23 NCV

March

14 Monday

_____

_____

_____

_____

15 Tuesday

_____

_____

_____

_____

16 Wednesday

_____

_____

_____

_____

Friday 18

Saturday 19

Palm Sunday / Spring Equinox **Sunday** 20

---

*S*erve God by doing common actions in a heavenly spirit,
and then, if your daily calling only leaves you cracks and
crevices of time, fill them up with holy service.

CHARLES SPURGEON

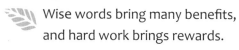 Wise words bring many benefits,
and hard work brings rewards.

Proverbs 12:14 NLT

21 Monday

22 Tuesday

23 Wednesday

Thursday 24

Friday 25

Saturday 26

Easter Sunday Sunday 27

*God does not give us everything we want,
but He does fulfill His promises, leading us along
the best and straightest paths to Himself.*

DIETRICH BONHOEFFER

April
2016

I long to give my best to life each day

and life itself longs not to live halfway

A perfect life is not what God requires

but fine-tuned faith, perfected through life's fires

Each job I do should hone my talents more

improving me, compelling me to soar

Lord, let me beget caliber each day

unparalleled, with excellence, I pray

S	M	T	W	T	F	S
					1	2
3	4	5	6	7	8	9
10	11	12	13	14	15	16
17	18	19	20	21	22	23
24	25	26	27	28	29	30

My daughter, do not fear. I will do for you whatever you ask, for all my people in the city know that you are a woman of excellence.

RUTH 3:11 NASB

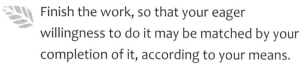 Finish the work, so that your eager willingness to do it may be matched by your completion of it, according to your means.

2 Corinthians 8:11 NIV

March/April

28 Monday

_____
_____
_____
_____

29 Tuesday

_____
_____
_____
_____

30 Wednesday

_____
_____
_____
_____

Thursday 31

Friday 1

Saturday 2

Sunday 3

*Never give up, for that is just the place and time
that the tide will turn.*

HARRIET BEECHER STOWE

> Pay careful attention to your own work,
> for then you will get the satisfaction of
> a job well done, and you won't need to
> compare yourself to anyone else. For we
> are each responsible for our own conduct.
>
> *Galatians 6:4-5 NLT*

April

4 Monday

_____

_____

_____

_____

_____

5 Tuesday

_____

_____

_____

_____

_____

6 Wednesday

_____

_____

_____

_____

_____

Thursday 7

Friday 8

Saturday 9

Sunday 10

Success doesn't just happen. It's planned for.

The humble will see their
God at work and be glad.
Let all who seek
God's help be encouraged.

Psalm 69:32 NLT

April

11 Monday

_____
_____
_____
_____
_____

12 Tuesday

_____
_____
_____
_____
_____

13 Wednesday

_____
_____
_____
_____
_____

Thursday 14

Friday 15

Saturday 16

Sunday 17

What then is time? If no one asks me, I know what it is.

If I wish to explain it to him who asks, I do not know.

AUGUSTINE

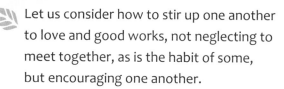

Let us consider how to stir up one another to love and good works, not neglecting to meet together, as is the habit of some, but encouraging one another.

Hebrews 10:24-25 ESV

April

18 Monday

_____

_____

_____

_____

19 Tuesday

_____

_____

_____

_____

20 Wednesday

_____

_____

_____

_____

_____

Thursday 21

First Day of Passover Friday 22

Saturday 23

Sunday 24

Peace if possible; truth at all costs.

MARTIN LUTHER

Every good gift and every perfect gift is from above, coming down from the Father of lights with whom there is no variation or shadow due to change.

James 1:17 ESV

April/May

25 Monday

_____
_____
_____
_____

26 Tuesday

_____
_____
_____
_____

27 Wednesday

_____
_____
_____
_____

Thursday 28

Friday 29

Last Day of Passover **Saturday** 30

Sunday 1

As much as you want to plan your life, it has a way of surprising you with unexpected things that can make you happier than you originally planned. That's what you call God's will.

May
2016

One vision for always to sing and to scream

A thousand bare petals, we garden and dream

In summer, in winter, the sun and the moon

Eternity shines, not a moment too soon

S	M	T	W	T	F	S
1	2	3	4	5	6	7
8	9	10	11	12	13	14
15	16	17	18	19	20	21
22	23	24	25	26	27	28
29	30	31				

"God is spirit, and those who worship him must worship in spirit and truth."

JOHN 4:24 NRSV

I will tell of the kindnesses of the LORD,
the deeds for which he is to be praised,
according to all the LORD has done for us...
according to his compassion and many kindnesses.

Isaiah 63:7 NIV

May

2   Monday

_____

_____

_____

_____

3   Tuesday

_____

_____

_____

_____

4   Wednesday

_____

_____

_____

_____

_____
_____
_____
_____

Friday 6

_____
_____
_____
_____

Saturday 7

_____
_____

Mother's Day **Sunday** 8

_____
_____
_____

Every day may not be good,

but there's something good in every day.

We are God's handiwork, created in
Christ Jesus to do good works, which
God prepared in advance for us to do.

Ephesians 2:10 NIV

May

9 Monday

10 Tuesday

11 Wednesday

Thursday 12

Friday 13

Saturday 14

Pentecost **Sunday 15**

*R*efuse to be average.

Let your heart soar as high as it will.

A.W. TOZER

It is more blessed to give than to receive.

Acts 20:35 NIV

May

16 Monday

_____

_____

_____

_____

17 Tuesday

_____

_____

_____

_____

18 Wednesday

_____

_____

_____

_____

_____

Thursday 19

Friday 20

Saturday 21

Sunday 22

The greatest form of praise is the sound of consecrated feet seeking out the lost and helpless.

BILLY GRAHAM

When you turn to the right or to the left,
your ears will hear a voice behind you,
saying, "This is the way; walk in it."

Isaiah 30:21 NIV

May

23 Monday

24 Tuesday

25 Wednesday

Thursday 26

_____

_____

_____

_____

Friday 27

_____

_____

_____

_____

Saturday 28

_____

_____

Sunday 29

_____

_____

_____

Life is only travelled once.

Today's moment becomes tomorrow's memory.

Enjoy every moment, good or bad,

because the gift of life is life itself.

June
2016

My heart defers to You, God

conforming to Your Word

It tethers me consistently

to vows You've overheard

Convict my wandering feet, Lord

and teach them to obey

So that I hear You call me

and run without delay

S	M	T	W	T	F	S
			1	2	3	4
5	6	7	8	9	10	11
12	13	14	15	16	17	18
19	20	21	22	23	24	25
26	27	28	29	30		

Surely, to obey is better than sacrifice.

1 SAMUEL 15:22 NRSV

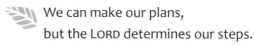

We can make our plans,
but the LORD determines our steps.

Proverbs 16:9 NLT

May/June

30 Monday *Memorial Day*

_____
_____
_____
_____

31 Tuesday

_____
_____
_____
_____

1 Wednesday

_____
_____
_____
_____
_____

Thursday 2

_____
_____
_____
_____
_____

Friday 3

_____
_____
_____
_____

Saturday 4

_____
_____

Sunday 5

_____
_____
_____

Don't wait for the perfect moment;

take the moment and make it perfect.

Guide me in your truth and teach me,
for you are God my Savior,
and my hope is in you all day long.

Psalm 25:5 NIV

June

6 Monday

_____
_____
_____
_____

7 Tuesday

_____
_____
_____
_____

8 Wednesday

_____
_____
_____
_____

Thursday 9

Friday 10

Saturday 11

Sunday 12

*know not the way God leads me,
but well I do know my Guide.*

MARTIN LUTHER

Trust in the LORD with all your heart,
And lean not on your own understanding;
In all your ways acknowledge Him,
and He shall direct your paths.

Proverbs 3:5-6 NKJV

June

13 Monday

_____
_____
_____
_____

14 Tuesday *Flag Day*

_____
_____
_____
_____

15 Wednesday

_____
_____
_____
_____

Thursday 16

_____
_____
_____
_____
_____

Friday 17

_____
_____
_____
_____
_____

Saturday 18

_____
_____
_____

Father's Day **Sunday** 19

_____
_____
_____

*If you worry about yesterday's failures,
then today's successes will be few.*

Listen to advice and accept discipline, and at the end you will be counted among the wise.

Proverbs 19:20 NIV

June

20 Monday Summer Solstice

21 Tuesday

22 Wednesday

Thursday 23

Friday 24

Saturday 25

Sunday 26

*Ask what Time is, it is nothing else but something of
eternal duration become finite, measurable and transitory.*

WILLIAM LAW

July

2016

Honor isn't just esteem we know we should be giving

It's honest, brave integrity that infiltrates our living

It's holding fast to principles and goodness at all cost

It's guarding reputation so no character is lost

S	M	T	W	T	F	S
					1	2
3	4	5	6	7	8	9
10	11	12	13	14	15	16
17	18	19	20	21	22	23
24	25	26	27	28	29	30
31						

*The wise will inherit honor,
but fools get disgrace.*

PROVERBS 3:35 ESV

May you be filled with joy, always thanking the Father. He has enabled you to share in the inheritance that belongs to his people, who live in the light.

Colossians 1:11-12 NLT

June/July

27   Monday

_____
_____
_____
_____

28   Tuesday

_____
_____
_____
_____
_____

29   Wednesday

_____
_____
_____
_____
_____

Thursday 30

_____
_____
_____
_____

Friday 1

_____
_____
_____
_____

Saturday 2

_____
_____

Sunday 3

_____
_____
_____

Perhaps it takes a purer faith to praise God
for unrealized blessings than for those we once
enjoyed or those we enjoy now.

A.W. TOZER

**The Lord has done great things for us,
and we are filled with joy.**

Psalm 126:3 NIV

July

4   **Monday**   *Independence Day*

_____
_____
_____
_____

5   **Tuesday**

_____
_____
_____
_____

6   **Wednesday**

_____
_____
_____
_____
_____

Thursday 7

_____
_____
_____
_____
_____

Friday 8

_____
_____
_____
_____

Saturday 9

_____
_____

Sunday 10

_____
_____
_____

Life is not measured by the number of breaths we take,

but by the number of moments that take our breath away.

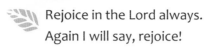

Rejoice in the Lord always.
Again I will say, rejoice!

Philippians 4:4 NKJV

July

11 Monday

_____

_____

_____

_____

12 Tuesday

_____

_____

_____

_____

13 Wednesday

_____

_____

_____

_____

_____

Thursday 14

_____
_____
_____
_____

Friday 15

_____
_____
_____
_____

Saturday 16

_____
_____

Sunday 17

_____
_____
_____

You haven't failed until you quit trying.

The world and its desires pass away, but whoever does the will of God lives forever.

1 John 2:17 NIV

July

18   Monday

_____
_____
_____
_____

19   Tuesday

_____
_____
_____
_____

20   Wednesday

_____
_____
_____
_____

Thursday 21

_____
_____
_____
_____
_____

Friday 22

_____
_____
_____
_____

Saturday 23

_____
_____

Sunday 24

_____
_____
_____

We need never shout across the spaces to an absent God. He is nearer than our own soul, closer than our most secret thoughts.

A.W. TOZER

We fix our eyes not on what is seen, but on what is unseen, since what is seen is temporary, but what is unseen is eternal.

2 Corinthians 4:18 NIV

July

25 Monday

_____

_____

_____

_____

26 Tuesday

_____

_____

_____

_____

27 Wednesday

_____

_____

_____

_____

Thursday 28

Friday 29

Saturday 30

Sunday 31

$\mathcal{M}$*y life will be the best illustration of all my work.*

HANS CHRISTIAN ANDERSON

August
2016

It takes faith to tie shoes or move mountains

Even with it, some days just ain't fun

But you won't win big races

without faith or tied laces

so get up and thank God you can run!

S	M	T	W	T	F	S
	1	2	3	4	5	6
7	8	9	10	11	12	13
14	15	16	17	18	19	20
21	22	23	24	25	26	27
28	29	30	31			

For you have need of endurance, so that after you have done the will of God, you may receive the promise.

HEBREWS 10:36, NKJV

The LORD is good to those whose hope is in him,
to the one who seeks him.

Lamentations 3:25 NIV

August

1 Monday

_____

_____

_____

_____

2 Tuesday

_____

_____

_____

_____

3 Wednesday

_____

_____

_____

_____

_____
_____
_____
_____
_____

_____
_____
_____
_____

_____
_____
_____

_____
_____
_____

Forgiveness does not change the past,

but it does change the future.

May the God of hope fill you will all joy and
peace as you trust in him, so that you may
overflow with hope by the power of the
Holy Spirit.

Romans 15:13 NIV

August

8   Monday

_____

_____

_____

_____

_____

9   Tuesday

_____

_____

_____

_____

_____

10   Wednesday

_____

_____

_____

_____

_____

Thursday 11

_____

_____

_____

_____

_____

Friday 12

_____

_____

_____

_____

_____

Saturday 13

_____

_____

_____

Sunday 14

_____

_____

_____

$\mathcal{T}$*his is true faith:*

a living confidence in the goodness of God.

MARTIN LUTHER

The precepts of the LORD are right,
giving joy to the heart.
The commands of the LORD are radiant,
giving light to the eyes.

Psalm 19:8 NIV

August

15   Monday

_____
_____
_____
_____

16   Tuesday

_____
_____
_____
_____

17   Wednesday

_____
_____
_____
_____

Thursday 18

_____
_____
_____
_____
_____

Friday 19

_____
_____
_____
_____

Saturday 20

_____
_____

Sunday 21

_____
_____
_____

Nothing is well done without prayer for the simple reason that it leaves God out of the account.

E.M. BOUNDS

Satisfy us in the morning
with your unfailing love,
that we may sing for joy
and be glad all our days.

Psalm 90:14 NIV

August

22 Monday

_____
_____
_____
_____
_____

23 Tuesday

_____
_____
_____
_____
_____

24 Wednesday

_____
_____
_____
_____
_____

Thursday 25

Friday 26

Saturday 27

Sunday 28

Life is the art of drawing without an eraser.

September

2016

Slow and steady wins the race

but can't we please pick up the pace?

It seems we're always pushing through

and answers seem long overdue

The world is moving, rushing by

and patience is in short supply

But when I stop within the crowd

I see the peace you live out loud

S	M	T	W	T	F	S
				1	2	3
4	5	6	7	8	9	10
11	12	13	14	15	16	17
18	19	20	21	22	23	24
25	26	27	28	29	30	

Stand firm, and you will win life.

LUKE 21:19 NIV

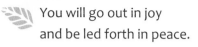

You will go out in joy
and be led forth in peace.

Isaiah 55:12 NIV

August/September

29 Monday

_____
_____
_____
_____

30 Tuesday

_____
_____
_____
_____

31 Wednesday

_____
_____
_____
_____

Thursday 1

Friday 2

Saturday 3

Sunday 4

It is not how much we have, but how much we enjoy, that makes happiness.

CHARLES SPURGEON

"For I know the plans I have for you,"
declares the LORD,
"plans to prosper you and not to harm you,
plans to give you hope and a future."

Jeremiah 29:11 NIV

September

5 Monday *Labor Day*

6 Tuesday

7 Wednesday

Thursday 8

Friday 9

Saturday 10

Sunday 11

Faith is not knowing what the future holds,

but knowing who holds the future.

O LORD, You have searched me and known me.
You know my sitting down and my rising up.

Psalm 139:1 NKJV

September

12 Monday

_____

_____

_____

_____

_____

13 Tuesday

_____

_____

_____

_____

_____

14 Wednesday

_____

_____

_____

_____

_____

_____

_____

_____

_____

_____

_____

_____

_____

_____

_____

_____

_____

_____

_____

Trials teach us what we are; they dig up the soil, and let us see what we are made of.

CHARLES SPURGEON

The steadfast love of the LORD never ceases;
his mercies never come to an end.

Lamentations 3:22 ESV

September

19 Monday

20 Tuesday

21 Wednesday

_____
_____
_____
_____
_____

Friday 23

_____
_____
_____
_____

Saturday 24

_____
_____

Sunday 25

_____
_____
_____

Those who walk with God always reach their destination.

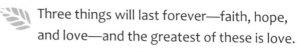

Three things will last forever—faith, hope, and love—and the greatest of these is love.

1 Corinthians 13:13 NLT

September/October

26 Monday

27 Tuesday

28 Wednesday

Thursday 29

_____
_____
_____
_____
_____

Friday 30

_____
_____
_____
_____
_____

Saturday 1

_____
_____
_____

Rosh Hashanah begins **Sunday** 2

_____
_____
_____

Nothing teaches us the preciousness of the Creator as much as when we learn the emptiness of everything else.

CHARLES SPURGEON

October

2016

Keep right on persevering;

you dare not give up now

Keep going strong, before too long

you'll get to take your bow!

S	M	T	W	T	F	S
						1
2	3	4	5	6	7	8
9	10	11	12	13	14	15
16	17	18	19	20	21	22
23	24	25	26	27	28	29
30	31					

*P*ray in the Spirit at all times with all kinds of prayers, asking for everything you need. To do this you must always be ready and never give up. Always pray for all God's people.

EPHESIANS 6:18 NCV

Sin shall no longer be your master, because you are not under the law, but under grace.

Romans 6:14 NIV

October

3 Monday

4 Tuesday *Rosh Hashanah ends*

5 Wednesday

Thursday 6

Friday 7

Saturday 8

Sunday 9

Faith is a living, daring confidence in God's grace, so sure and certain that a man could stake his life on it a thousand times.

MARTIN LUTHER

I urge you to live a life worthy of the calling
you have received.

Ephesians 4:1 NIV

October

10 Monday *Columbus Day*

_____
_____
_____
_____
_____

11 Tuesday *Yom Kippur begins*

_____
_____
_____
_____
_____

12 Wednesday *Yom Kippur ends*

_____
_____
_____
_____
_____

Thursday 13

Friday 14

Saturday 15

Sunday 16

The highest form of worship is the worship of unselfish service.

BILLY GRAHAM

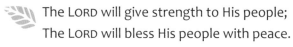

The LORD will give strength to His people;
The LORD will bless His people with peace.

Psalm 29:11 NKJV

October

17 Monday

_____
_____
_____
_____

18 Tuesday

_____
_____
_____
_____

19 Wednesday

_____
_____
_____
_____

Thursday 20

_____

_____

_____

_____

_____

Friday 21

_____

_____

_____

_____

Saturday 22

_____

_____

_____

Sunday 23

_____

_____

_____

*The way to do a great deal is to keep on doing a little.
The way to do nothing at all is to be continually resolving
that you will do everything.*

CHARLES SPURGEON

Those who love your instructions
have great peace
and do not stumble.

Psalm 119:165 NLT

October

24 Monday

_____
_____
_____
_____
_____

25 Tuesday

_____
_____
_____
_____
_____

26 Wednesday

_____
_____
_____
_____
_____

_____

_____

_____

_____

_____

Friday 28

_____

_____

_____

_____

_____

Saturday 29

_____

_____

_____

Sunday 30

_____

_____

_____

Choice, not circumstances, determines your success.

November

2016

I'd cause myself less trouble

and I'd spare my heart some aches

If I would count my blessings

and stop numbering mistakes

To live like I'm indebted,

to God and those I love

Would bring me double blessings

that I'd be more worthy of

S	M	T	W	T	F	S
		1	2	3	4	5
6	7	8	9	10	11	12
13	14	15	16	17	18	19
20	21	22	23	24	25	26
27	28	29	30			

Since we receive a kingdom which
cannot be shaken, let us show
gratitude, by which we may offer
to God an acceptable service with
reverence and awe.

HEBREWS 12:28 NASB

Do not be unwise, but understand what the will of the Lord is.

Ephesians 5:17 NKJV

October/November

31 Monday

_____

_____

_____

_____

1 Tuesday

_____

_____

_____

_____

2 Wednesday

_____

_____

_____

_____

Thursday 3

_____
_____
_____
_____

Friday 4

_____
_____
_____
_____

Saturday 5

_____
_____
_____

Daylight Savings Time ends **Sunday** 6

_____
_____
_____

Never get tired of doing little things for others.

Sometimes those little things occupy

the biggest part of their hearts.

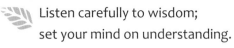

Listen carefully to wisdom;
set your mind on understanding.

Proverbs 2:2 NCV

November

7 Monday

8 Tuesday *Election Day*

9 Wednesday

Thursday 10

Veterans' Day Friday 11

Saturday 12

Sunday 13

I have held many things in my hands, and I have lost them all;

but whatever I have placed in God's hands, that I still possess.

MARTIN LUTHER

Let us not grow weary of doing good,
for in due season we will reap,
if we do not give up.

Galatians 6:9 ESV

November

14 Monday

15 Tuesday

16 Wednesday

Thursday 17

_____
_____
_____
_____
_____

Friday 18

_____
_____
_____
_____
_____

Saturday 19

_____
_____

Sunday 20

_____
_____
_____

Faith is to believe what we do not see, and the reward

of this is to see what we believe.

AUGUSTINE

My voice You shall hear in the morning, O LORD;
In the morning I will direct it to You,
And I will look up.

Psalm 5:3 NKJV

November

21   Monday

_____
_____
_____
_____
_____

22   Tuesday

_____
_____
_____
_____
_____

23   Wednesday

_____
_____
_____
_____
_____

First Sunday of Advent **Thursday** 24

_____
_____
_____
_____
_____

Friday 25

_____
_____
_____
_____
_____

Saturday 26

_____
_____
_____

Thanksgiving Day **Sunday** 27

_____
_____
_____

There are two days in my calendar: This day and that Day.

MARTIN LUTHER

December

2016

So burn like a fire!

Intense, even higher!

Your life is God's gift to His earth!

Burn strong, grow in grace

put faith on your face

then watch and you'll learn what you're worth

S	M	T	W	T	F	S
				1	2	3
4	5	6	7	8	9	10
11	12	13	14	15	16	17
18	19	20	21	22	23	24
25	26	27	28	29	30	31

Never be lacking in zeal, but keep your spiritual fervor, serving the Lord.

ROMANS 12:11 NIV

To do what is right and just is more
acceptable to the LORD than sacrifice.

Proverbs 21:3 NIV

November/December

28 Monday

_____

_____

_____

_____

29 Tuesday

_____

_____

_____

_____

30 Wednesday

_____

_____

_____

_____

Thursday 1

Friday 2

Saturday 3

Sunday 4

What you are is God's gift to you.

What you become is your gift to God.

Examine everything carefully; hold fast to that which is good; abstain from every form of evil.

1 Thessalonians 5:21-22 NASB

December

5 Monday

6 Tuesday

7 Wednesday

Thursday 8

Friday 9

Saturday 10

Sunday 11

Aim at heaven and you will get earth thrown in.

Aim at earth and you get neither.

C.S. LEWIS

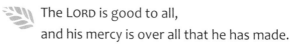

The LORD is good to all,
and his mercy is over all that he has made.

Psalm 145:9 ESV

December

12 Monday

_____
_____
_____
_____
_____

13 Tuesday

_____
_____
_____
_____
_____

14 Wednesday

_____
_____
_____
_____
_____

Thursday 15

Friday 16

Saturday 17

Sunday 18

Happiness will never come to those who don't appreciate what they already have.

"Whoever wants to save their life will lose it,
but whoever loses their life for me will find it."

Matthew 16:25 NIV

December

19   Monday

_____

_____

_____

_____

20   Tuesday

_____

_____

_____

_____

21   Wednesday   *Winter Solstice*

_____

_____

_____

_____

Thursday 22

Friday 23

Christmas Eve **Saturday** 24

Christmas Day / Hanukkah begins **Sunday** 25

The Christian life is a life of paradoxes. We must give to receive, realize we are blind to see, become simple to be wise, suffer for gain, and die to live.

By day the Lord directs his love,
at night his song is with me—
a prayer to the God of my life.

Psalm 42:8 NIV

December

26 Monday

_____
_____
_____
_____

27 Tuesday

_____
_____
_____
_____

28 Wednesday

_____
_____
_____
_____

Thursday 29

_____
_____
_____
_____
_____

Friday 30

_____
_____
_____
_____
_____

New Year's Eve **Saturday** 31

_____
_____

New Year's Day **Sunday** 1

_____
_____
_____

*G*etting on your knees keeps you from falling.

Belle City Gifts
Racine, Wisconsin, USA

Belle City Gifts is an imprint of BroadStreet Publishing Group LLC.
Broadstreetpublishing.com

Growing in Grace 2016 PLANNER

© 2015 by BroadStreet Publishing

ISBN 978-1-4245-5069-2

Month-at-a-glance poems composed by Laura Harris Smith from the *Growing in Grace Devotional Journal*. Used with permission. Other unattributed quotations are from anonymous authors. Interior flower image by Jeorgi Smith at www.jeorgimages.com.

Scripture quotations marked (NLT) are taken from the Holy Bible, New Living Translation, copyright © 1996, 2004, 2007. Used by permission of Tyndale House Publishers, Inc., Carol Stream, Illinois 60188. All rights reserved. Scripture quotations marked (NIV) are taken from the Holy Bible, New International Version®, NIV®. Copyright © 1973, 1978, 1984, 2011 by Biblica, Inc.™ Used by permission of Zondervan. All rights reserved worldwide. www.zondervan.com. The "NIV" and "New International Version" are trademarks registered in the United States Patent and Trademark Office by Biblica, Inc.™ Scripture quotations marked (NCV) are taken from the New Century Version®. Copyright © 2005 by Thomas Nelson. Used by permission. All rights reserved. Scripture quotations marked (NASB) are taken from the New American Standard Bible®, Copyright © 1960, 1962, 1963, 1968, 1971, 1972, 1973, 1975, 1977, 1995 by The Lockman Foundation. Used by permission. www.Lockman. org. Scripture quotations marked (NRSV) are taken from the New Revised Standard Version Bible, copyright 1989, Division of Christian Education of the National Council of the Churches of Christ in the United States of America. Used by permission. All rights reserved. Scripture quotations marked (ESV) are from the ESV® Bible (The Holy Bible, English Standard Version®), copyright © 2001 by Crossway, a publishing ministry of Good News Publishers. Used by permission. All rights reserved. Scripture quotations marked (TLB) are taken from The Living Bible copyright © 1971. Used by permission of Tyndale House Publishers, Inc., Carol Stream, Illinois 60188. All rights reserved. Scripture quotations marked (NKJV) are taken from the New King James Version®. Copyright © 1982 by Thomas Nelson. Used by permission. All rights reserved. Scripture quotations marked (TPT) are taken from The Passion Translation® of the Holy Bible. Copyright © 2014, 2015 by BroadStreet Publishing. All rights reserved.

Design by Chris Garborg | www.garborgdesign.com
Compiled and edited by Michelle Winger | www.literallyprecise.com

Printed in China.

15   16   17   18   19   20   21   7   6   5   4   3   2   1

If you enjoyed the poetry in this planner and would like to dive in a little deeper, check out the *Growing in Grace* devotional journal.

All that God creates flourishes and multiplies. Growth is God's idea and He is your source of grace for all your heart encounters each day. Experience God's unfailing love as you mature in sixty-four life-giving themes. God is able to make all grace abound to you so that you can thrive in every good work.

ISBN: 978-1-4245-4996-2

- 6 x 8 hardcover
- 144 pages
- textured debossing and spot UV on cover
- high quality paper with lightly ruled lines for journaling
- full color interior
- elastic band
- ribbon marker

Available at Amazon.com, BN.com, and Christianbook.com.

ABOUT THE AUTHOR

LAURA HARRIS SMITH lives in Nashville, Tennessee, where she and her husband, Chris, pastor Eastgate Creative Christian Fellowship. Laura is the founder and director of the Eastgate Creative Arts Conservatory, where she mentors young writers from all over the world in her online writing courses. Laura is the author of numerous books, including *Seeing the Voice of God: What God is Telling You Through Dreams and Visions*, which topped the charts at #1 on the Amazon Best Sellers List in several Christian categories. She speaks and ministers nationally and internationally across denominational lines and is known for bringing a light-hearted look to the heaviest of biblical topics. Her presentations always include her entertaining poetry. Married for over thirty years, Chris and Laura have six children. With half of them now grown and married, they have a growing list of grandchildren that outnumbers the kids. Invite Laura to speak at booking@ LauraHarrisSmith.com. Learn more about Laura's ministry at www.LauraHarrisSmith.com or www.EastgateCCF.com.